P9-DGV-905

LEGENDS
OF THE WEST

The Black Cowboys

Butch Cassidy

Wyatt Earp

The Gunslingers

Jesse James

Annie Oakley

LEGENDS OF THE WEST

ANNIE OAKLEY

John Wukovits

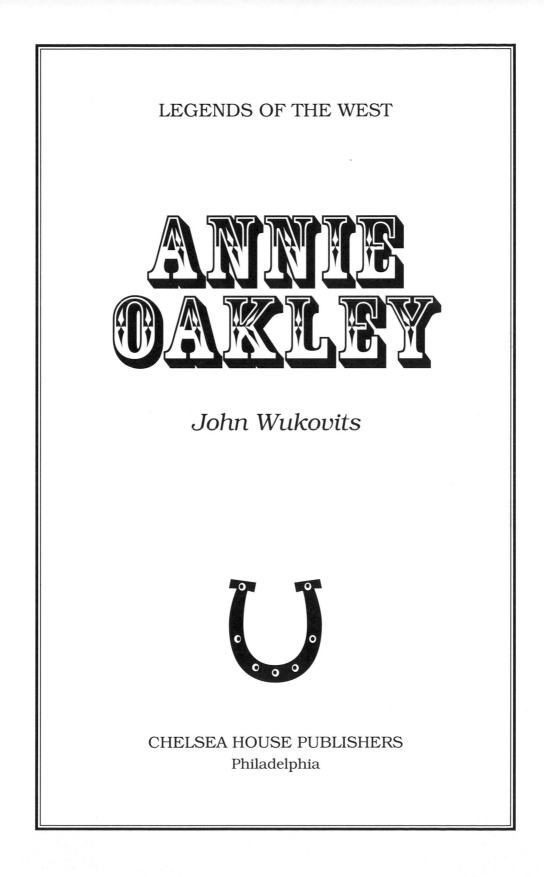

CHELSEA HOUSE PUBLISHERS
Philadelphia

Chelsea House Publishers

Staff for **ANNIE OAKLEY**
Cover Design and Digital Illustration: Alison Burnside
Cover Portrait Credit: Western History Department, Denver Public Library
Picture Researcher: John F. Wukovits

First Printing

1 3 5 7 9 8 6 4 2

For Terri—like Annie, another wonderful lady

Library of Congress Cataloging-in-Publication Data

Wukovits, John F., 1944-
        Annie Oakley/John Wukovits.
            p. cm. — (Legends of the West)
Includes bibliographical references and index.
Summary: Recounts the life of the markswoman and performer who achieved fame
with Buffalo Bill Cody's Wild West Show.
        ISBN 0-7910-3906-4 (hc)
1. Oakley, Annie, 1860-1926.—Juvenile literature. 2. Shooters of firearms—United States—
Biography—Juvenile literature. 3. Frontier and pioneer life—West (U.S.)—Juvenile literature.
[1. Oakley, Annie, 1860-1926. 2. Sharpshooters. 3. Entertainers. 4. Women—Biography.] I.
Title. II. Series.
GV1157.03W85   1997
799.3'092—dc21
[B]   97-9106
                                                                                          CIP
                                                                                           AC

CONTENTS

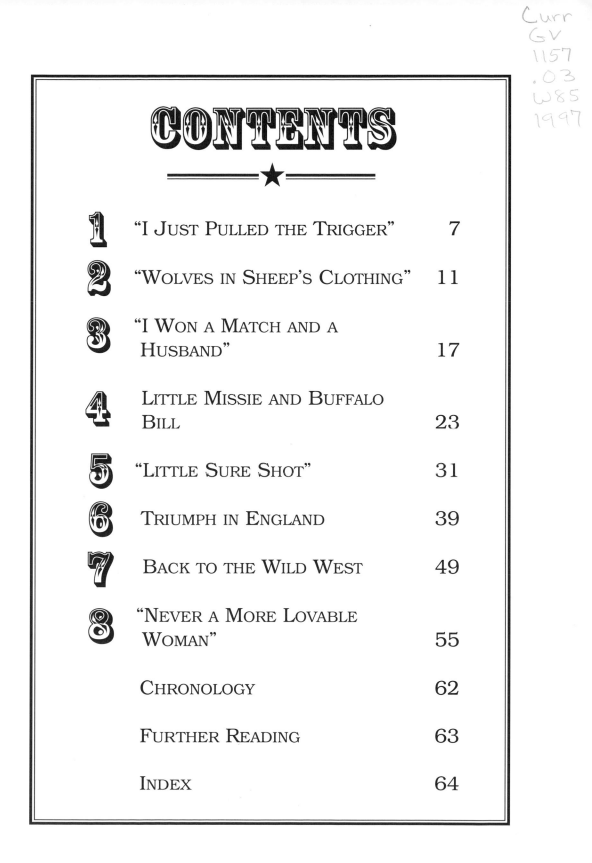

───── ★ ─────

GRAY PHOTO
BOSTON.

ANNIE OAKLEY

"I Just Pulled the Trigger"

Jacob and Susan Moses loaded their children onto a wagon and joined the steady stream of travelers heading west from Pennsylvania to Ohio. Strangely, they now slowly lumbered along the same road that had given them an income and home, for the two Quaker parents had operated a thriving wagoners' inn along the much-used route. That is, until a fire destroyed the inn and most of what the young couple owned.

Instead of complaining about their bad fortune, Jacob and Susan decided to move west and start a farm in Ohio. No sense worrying about the past, they reasoned. All that did was bring lots of heartache and no solutions. Better to concentrate on starting over and, with their typical hard work and optimism, before long the family would once more prosper.

Annie's comfort and ease with rifles and shotguns started at an early age and lasted throughout her lifetime.

So, as the 1850s drew to a close, they settled on rolling farmland in North Star, a Darke County township situated in southwest Ohio about eighty miles from Cincinnati. They required plenty of land to grow crops, both for market and for themselves, since within a few years the family expanded to seven children.

One daughter was marked for fame. Born on August 13, 1860, Annie Moses loved to roam the open fields near her home, where she and her three older sisters collected hickory nuts, climbed trees, and watched small animals scurry away at their approach. There was little to equal the joy Annie received from being in fresh air and scampering about fertile farmland.

Sadly, tragedy hit twice in succession and threw young Annie's world into a tailspin. In 1866, when Annie was just six years old, Jacob died of illness. Within one year her oldest sister, Mary Jane, passed away when she could not recover from a dangerous bout of pneumonia. A happy, carefree existence suddenly changed into a dark nightmare for the little girl, who dearly loved her father and sister.

But the family had to carry on, so Susan did her best to hold the clan together. Annie, a small, slim girl with keen eyes who sported chestnut hair that fell to her shoulders, completed her chores around the cabin without complaint, but she missed Jacob and Mary Jane. She wished she could help her mother in other ways besides simply doing chores.

One day when Annie was nine years old, she stared at a rifle that was mounted above the fireplace. Though she had never fired a gun, she had often watched her father load and shoot when he went hunting, and she felt confident that she could do the same. Maybe this was a way she could help her overburdened mother, who was then on a nursing trip into a neighboring home to bring in sorely needed money.

Annie stepped onto a chair, lifted the long rifle off its supports, and loaded it with what she thought would be the correct amount of gunpowder and shot.

"Stand back, John," she muttered after she and her younger brother ran outside to test the weapon. Quickly spotting a squirrel, Annie awkwardly raised the heavy gun and took careful aim. "It's going to be squirrel pie for supper tonight!"

Annie's first shot went high and wide, but she never saw its path because the force of the explosion knocked her backward onto the ground. She had put too much gunpowder in the weapon. Dazed but unhurt from her first encounter with a gun, Annie dusted herself off and decided she had a lot to learn about rifles before using one.

Over the following months she practiced with the weapon and discovered that accurate shooting came easy to her. After Annie brought home a turkey, which she had shot clean through the head, her mother asked, "How did you do it, Annie?"

"It was easy," she replied. "When it felt right, I just pulled the trigger."

Annie was comfortable using a rifle, and she was happy that because of her skill, the family ate better. This was only the beginning of a long association between Annie and her rifle.

Before that began, however, sadness once again slapped the young girl in the face.

Though her early life contained sorrow, a young Annie's face mirrored tenderness and warmth.

"Wolves in Sheep's Clothing"

Struggle as hard as she could, Susan could not support the entire family by herself. Though she hated to do it, in 1869 Susan had no choice but to split the family. Neighbors took in some of the children, but the only place she could find for nine-year-old Annie was the Darke County Infirmary, a home run by Crawford Eddington and his wife for orphans, the mentally ill, or those too poor, sick, or old to care for themselves. Annie reacted in terror at the thought of leaving her family and living in an orphanage with strange children.

"For how long?" wondered the shocked girl.

"Not long," replied her mother. "A few weeks...a month, perhaps. Until we have a little more money."

So in 1869 Annie packed her bags and left for what she hoped would be a brief stay at the

Before Annie found the happiness she so longed for, she had to endure turbulent years.

orphanage. As weeks stretched into months and the prospect of soon returning home dimmed, Annie became disheartened. Not only did she miss her family, but she hated the other children in the Darke County Infirmary, who viciously teased the quiet girl and made fun of her last name. "Moses Poses!" they cruelly shouted whenever Annie appeared. As a result, young Annie tried to keep out of everyone's way.

The next year a ray of hope appeared when a farmer and his wife rode to the orphanage. The man walked up to Mr. Eddington and explained, "I'm looking for a girl to live with my family. I will pay her 50 cents a week. She won't have much work to do, and she can go to school."

The Eddingtons wrote Susan who, pleased that her daughter would receive both an education and pay, gave permission for the couple to take in Annie. Delighted to be leaving the orphanage, Annie looked forward to a better life, though she preferred being home with her mother and family.

Her hopes for happiness were quickly dashed. As soon as the farmer and his wife arrived at their cabin with Annie, the woman barked to the ten-year-old, "You will rise at four a.m. to prepare breakfast. Biscuits, fired corn-meal mush, bacon, potatoes, and coffee." A stunned Annie could hardly believe what she was hearing, but it turned worse. "Then you will milk the cows and feed the pigs" in addition to doing the dishes, laundry, gathering vegetables, and caring for the couple's baby.

Trying to contain her tears, Annie glanced toward the man and asked, "My schoolbooks?"

"We will see about that," he answered in a gruff voice. Annie then realized that both she and the Eddingtons had been tricked.

Every day Annie finished her lengthy list of chores, tried to stay out of the couple's way, and hoped that her mother would rescue her from the misery. Unknown to Annie, Susan sent a letter to the couple stating that she needed her daughter back home, but the couple responded by lying that Annie was so happy with them that she preferred to stay where she was.

"The man was a brute and his wife a domineering woman," Annie wrote years later. She compared them to wolves in sheep's clothing—people who looked nice and offered happiness, then snatched it all away. She vowed never to speak their real names—a vow she kept her entire life—and instead thought of them as Mr. and Mrs. wolf, purposely using a small "w" as her way of insulting the mean couple.

Saddened by the situation, Annie waited for her chance to get away. The couple closely watched Annie and threatened to beat her if they thought she was up to anything suspicious, so she had to be extremely careful. Finally, her opportunity arrived. One night in 1872, as the exhausted couple slept soundly, Annie quietly slipped out of bed, crept out the door, and ran into the nearby woods. From there she headed to the closest town and boarded a train, which took her home.

A surprised Susan welcomed her daughter with open arms. Annie learned that her three older sisters were married and on their own, and that her mother had remarried—to a a tender, caring man man named Joseph Shaw who was delighted to have Annie with them. Called Grandpap Shaw by the children because he was ten years older than Susan, Shaw borrowed money to build a new home for the family.

Though Annie finally felt peace and contentment, she wished she could find a way to help Shaw pay off the huge loan. But what could a twelve-year-old girl do? Taking down her father's long-barreled cap-and-ball rifle, Annie headed to the fields to at least bring home game for the family's table.

Annie's skill as a marksman spread throughout the county and attracted the attention of two men. One, a businessman named Frenchy LaMotte, told her he would purchase any fur pelts she brought him. She struck a profitable deal with LaMotte, and even changed her last name from Moses, the subject of the orphans' taunts, to Mozee, which is what LaMotte called her.

Shortly after, another businessman named Charlie Katzenberger contacted her. He was impressed that Annie shot all her game through the head instead of in the body, which he knew made the game easier to prepare for eating. When he mentioned this, Annie told him, "I try to hit them in the head. That way no lead shots get in the meat. You could break a tooth if you bit into shot."

Katzenberger knew that Jack Frost, the manager of one of Cincinnati's finest establishments, the Bevis Hotel, would pay good money for Annie's game. It was sound business for Frost to ensure that his customers could eat without worrying about picking out pieces of shot or cracking a tooth, which meant that a handsome deal could be arranged between Katzenberger and the manager.

Annie jumped in excitement when Katzenberger explained the arrangement. She could finally help Shaw, and within a few years Annie had earned enough from her hunting to pay off the loan for her stepfather.

When Annie was sixteen, her older sister Lydia Stein wrote home asking if Annie could come live with her husband Joseph and her in Cincinnati. Sensing Annie's hesitation to again leave home, Susan mentioned she thought it was a good idea, then read part of Lydia's letter to her daughter, who had not yet learned to read.

"It is good for a girl to see the way people live in the city and not be always hunting in the woods. A girl can go to school here, even learn to make dresses and play the piano. Joe has a good job and we are in a nice house with a spare room for a little sister." Lydia ended the letter with a bit of advice. "You are sixteen now and ready for new things."

Annie agreed, and began preparations for a trip away from Darke County. She would not return for a long time.

By age 16, Annie had grown into a beautiful, though shy, girl. Living with her sister in Cincinnati would change her life more than she realized.

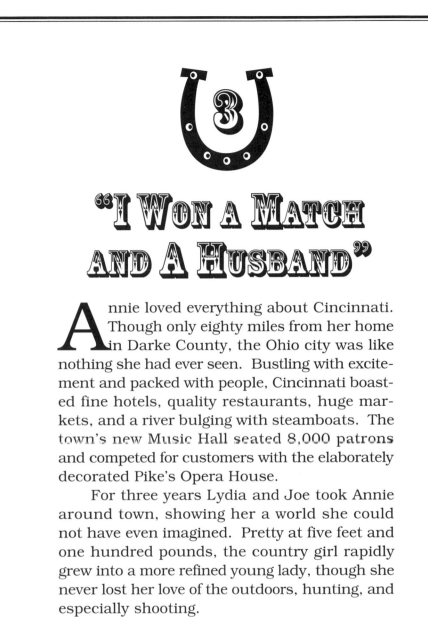

3

"I Won a Match and a Husband"

Annie loved everything about Cincinnati. Though only eighty miles from her home in Darke County, the Ohio city was like nothing she had ever seen. Bustling with excitement and packed with people, Cincinnati boasted fine hotels, quality restaurants, huge markets, and a river bulging with steamboats. The town's new Music Hall seated 8,000 patrons and competed for customers with the elaborately decorated Pike's Opera House.

For three years Lydia and Joe took Annie around town, showing her a world she could not have even imagined. Pretty at five feet and one hundred pounds, the country girl rapidly grew into a more refined young lady, though she never lost her love of the outdoors, hunting, and especially shooting.

In 1879 Joe Stein took Annie to Charlie

Annie found happiness in both an exciting career and a loving husband while in Cincinnati.

Stuttelberg's Shooting Gallery. After claiming to be a decent shot, Joe picked up a rifle, aimed at two rows of metal ducks and rabbits, and fired six shots in rapid succession. Two targets toppled over.

When he noticed a slight smile forming on Annie's face, Joe handed the rifle to her. "Do you think you can do any better?" he asked. Annie took careful aim, then knocked over the first five rabbits that came into view.

Watching from a distance, Charlie Stuttelberg was as impressed as Joe at the girl's evident skill with a rifle. He walked over, introduced himself, and wondered where she learned to handle a gun like that.

"Quail are harder to hit than a tin target," Annie responded.

"All right, girl, let's see you do that again," challenged Stuttelberg, still not convinced that luck had no part in the shooting. Six more targets passed in front of Annie; six targets shattered to pieces.

"You don't look like a marksman," shouted Stuttelberg, "but I'll bet you can outshoot Frank Butler."

"Who is that?" asked Annie.

"He's the shooting star at the Coliseum," replied Stuttelberg.

The three walked over to the elegant Bevis Hotel, managed by Jack Frost. Though he had purchased Annie's game through Charlie Katzenberger, Frost had never met Annie nor realized that his quality game had been provided by a girl. After being introduced to Annie by Stuttelberg, Frost knew he could make some fast money.

Frank Butler, of the Butler and Company shooting team, had brought his act to Cincinnati and was staying at the Bevis Hotel. After coming to the United States from Ireland in 1863, Butler worked odd jobs to earn money. Whenever he could, he practiced with his rifle. When he had saved enough, he took to the road and, over ten years, established a reputation for wizardry with a weapon. Wherever he stopped for exhibitions, Butler enjoyed meeting local marksmen in shooting contests, normally involving a significant amount of money for the winner and anyone who bet on him. Butler rarely lost.

Frost approached the marksman. "I've got a match for you, Frank. A hundred dollars says my shooter can beat you."

"Who is he?" wondered Butler, eager to accept another opportunity to pocket some easy money.

"Oh, just someone from up country. Not a name you'd know."

When the day arrived for the challenge, Butler searched the gathering crowd for signs of his opponent. No one attracted his attention except a young girl, who looked out of place in the throng of men.

"Who's the country girl?" he asked Frost.

"That's your opponent."

Butler checked his urge to snicker, but looked at Frost in an effort to determine if he was serious. When he saw that Frost did, indeed, plan to bet on this girl against him, Butler graciously welcomed her and started to get ready.

For the contest, Annie and Butler had to take turns shooting at clay pigeons, which were saucer-shaped pieces of clay. When the shooter cried, "Pull!" a machine hurled the pigeon into the air. The shooter had one shot to hit the

Frank Butler reacted like most men did when they first saw Annie with a gun--with a grin and a disbelieving attitude.

Frank showered his Annie with love. The two were never apart for the rest of their lives.

pigeon before it fell to the ground. Whoever knocked down the most clay pigeons won the contest.

A large crowd gathered, drawn by the matching of a world-class champion shooter and an unknown young girl. Butler stepped up, yelled "Pull!" and quickly demolished the first pigeon that soared above.

Most spectators expected Annie to be soundly trounced and sneered at the sight of such a small girl competing against Butler. Fully counting on her to miss her target, they hushed as Annie walked up.

"Pull!" yelled Annie. She carefully followed the small clay disk as it sped upward, slowly squeezed the trigger, and watched the pigeon break into pieces as her bullet tore through it.

Back and forth they went. Pigeon after pigeon Annie matched Butler, each time hearing louder applause from a disbelieving audience. Here was Frank Butler, champion shooter, being equalled by a girl!

Each shooter hit the first twelve targets. Frank stepped up for his 13th pigeon, still confident that he could best his unheralded opponent, but also impressed with her. She could shoot a gun with the best, and she was pretty as well.

"Pull!" The pigeon lofted upward seconds before Butler's shot shattered the stillness. A gasp of surprise sounded from the crowd as the target dropped untouched to the ground. He had missed.

Annie knew that if she hit her pigeon, she would win the match. Without waiting, she yelled "Pull!" aimed, and fired in one smooth motion, disintegrating the pigeon with a shot that caused an uproarious cheer from the throng and ended Butler's string of successes.

Rather than being upset over his defeat by a girl, Butler was captivated by his opponent. Certainly her skills impressed him, but he was more taken by her confidence. And for someone so pretty, he thought, to be such a fine shooter. This was no ordinary girl.

In the following days, Frank and Annie were rarely out of each other's company, filling their time together with walks, picnics, and hunting. They fell in love, and when Frank had to leave Cincinnati and travel to the next stop on his tour, he gave her a promise.

"Wait for me, Annie. I will be back in one year, and then I will have something to ask you."

Butler kept his word. One year later when his act returned to Cincinnati, he proposed to Annie. Though she first had to convince her mother that Butler was the right man—in those days show business people were looked down upon by many, and Butler was ten years older than Annie—she and Frank married in 1880.

As Annie loved to explain about the shooting contest in the years that followed, "I won a match and a husband."

LITTLE MISSIE
AND BUFFALO BILL

As her sister, Lydia, had shown to Annie the exciting world offered by Cincinnati, so now did Frank introduce her to an even bigger world, one that included not simply large cities, but states, nations, oceans, and continents. Annie, the little country hunter from Ohio, fit into this new circle as if she had been born for it.

For five years the couple traveled the Midwest states of Ohio, Indiana, Michigan, Illinois, and Wisconsin. At first Annie was a spectator, as Frank toured with his shooting partner, Billy Graham. Touted as "Graham & Butler, Rifle Team and Champion All-Around Shots," they dazzled crowds with their shooting expertise. Annie watched each performance, and soon she could execute every trick with as much skill as either Frank or Graham.

Annie's talent with a rifle packed arenas throughout the Midwest and captured the attention of famed Western hero, Buffalo Bill.

One night an ill Billy Graham had to withdraw from the performance, forcing Frank to look for a substitute. He had to search no farther than his wife.

"Billy can't be my partner tonight," he said to Annie. "You'll have to take his place."

Though Annie could equal Graham skill for skill, she had only done the tricks in practice fields, far from the critical eyes of paying customers. Could she do as well with hundreds, or even thousands, of people looking on?

"But I have never been on stage," she objected.

"That's nothing," Frank reassured her. "You've been watching every night. You know our act by heart. And you are a better shot than Billy."

Annie reluctantly agreed to replace Graham. Her nervousness increased when the audience groaned after learning that not only would Graham be missing from the show, but his place would be taken by a nineteen-year-old girl.

All her natural instincts, perfected by years of hunting in Ohio fields and woods, now took command. After joining her husband in the arena to minimal applause, Annie shattered target after target, each time receiving louder shouts from the audience. One trick that drew the audience to its feet began with Frank placing an apple on top of his dog's head. Frank had trained the dog, named George, to sit perfectly still for this portion of the act. As the audience hushed, worried for the dog's safety, Annie calmly took aim and knocked the apple clean off George's head. By the time the show ended, the audience cheered and stomped for more from this amazing girl.

Frank recognized that they had created something special and put Annie in the act permanently. He changed the act's name to "Butler & Butler" and placed the focus solely on his wife. While people in the Midwest had seen many male champion shooters, where else could they go to watch a five-feet, one-hundred pound female put on such a display of wizardry?

And so started a seemingly endless round of appearances in front of thunderous crowds. The job contained certain drawbacks, of course. After putting on as many as six shows a day, six days each week, Annie and Frank would hurriedly pack up, jump on yet another rail-road car, head to another city, and start all over again. Hotels could be dreary substitutes for home, and they could never count on home-cooked meals or permanent friends.

After Annie successfully filled in for Billy Graham, Frank installed her as the act's main attraction. He was content to assist her and to manage their careers.

Spectators loved Annie's hand-made costumes, which she made so that she would have freer movement of her arms and feet.

Still, they were together and having fun seeing different parts of the country. They met fascinating individuals and visited beautiful locales. For two people who had grown up poor, they began making more money than they had imagined, part of which Annie sent home to her mother. The couple grew closer each day and fell more in love. In fact, every day Frank read the newspaper to Annie, and slowly he taught her to read well enough so that she could digest the paper on her own.

They had a true family act. Annie sewed the costumes she wore for her performances, and soon audiences expected to see Annie ride out in her trademark loose-fitting blouses—she needed room to easily swing her arms around to the next target—and skirts that ended at the knees instead of the ankles to ensure free movement of the feet. About the only aspect that was not family was the act's name, which Frank changed to Butler & Oakley because some theater managers disliked booking family acts.

Gradually their fame grew. In April 1884 Annie received a fantastic offer to appear for forty weeks with the Sells Brothers Circus, one of the largest of the two hundred circuses that traveled the Midwest. Its owners boasted they had gathered a circus second to none and immodestly billed the show as:

> The Biggest of all Big Shows, requiring three immense railroad trains. Its parade a plume-topped tidal wave of splendor. Its menangerie filled with the finest collections of Carniverous and Herbivorous animals ever seen anywhere. Under its big top one hundred superior and startling acts at every performance.

Called at first "Butler and Oakley, the Famous Far West Champion Rifle Shots," the act was a sensation from its first night. Frank soon realized that the crowds flocked in to see Annie, so he turned it into a one-woman show. He concentrated on managing the act while his wife did all the shooting.

While they enjoyed their first year with Sells Brothers, Frank and Annie particularly looked ahead to the circus's December 1884 appearance in New Orleans, which would be hosting the World's Fair and Cotton Exposition. They knew that enormous crowds would pack their circus and every other show in town.

Instead, forty-four straight days of rain washed out the entire run. Disappointed, the two passed time by walking about the show's grounds, talking with each other, practicing their act, and reading.

One day they decided to look into the possibility of joining an even larger company than Sells Brothers—the famed Wild West Show. Headed by noted Western scout and Indian fighter William Cody—more commonly called Buffalo Bill—the show featured authentic cowboys, Western sheriffs, outlaws, and Indians.

Annie and Frank strolled into the tent of Buffalo Bill's general manager, Major John Burke. "Major," said Frank, "we're from the Sells Brothers Circus. We're wondering if you'd be interested in adding us to your show."

"I don't know," replied Burke. "Nothing much is happening now because of all the rain. What can you do?"

Frank explained their act, then had Annie run through part of her routine. Burke liked what he saw.

"We can't do anything now, because Cody

Buffalo Bill could spot a skilled marksmen with ease, and he knew he had one in this young girl.

is out of town. This spring the show will be in St. Louis, and if you can be there, you'll be able to talk to both Cody and his partner, Nate Salsbury."

"We'll be there, Major," answered Frank.

The next spring Annie put on another exhibition for Buffalo Bill and Salsbury, who instantly agreed this girl should become part of their act. Buffalo Bill stepped toward Annie and offered his hand.

"They've told me about you, Missie. We're glad to have you here."

After signing the contract, Buffalo Bill led Annie and Frank to the food tent, called for the workers' attention, and announced, "This little Missie is Annie Oakley. She's going to be shooting with us, and I want you boys to welcome her and treat her well."

From then on, Annie was called Missie by just about every worker in Buffalo Bill's Wild West Show. A successful seventeen-year association had begun.

"Little Sure Shot"

Annie nervously tugged at her blouse to get it just right. She wanted to look good for the large crowd—her first one for Buffalo Bill—but she also needed ease of movement so she could quickly aim at a series of targets. Nate Salsbury had printed hundreds of advertising posters proclaiming Annie as "The Peerless Wing and Rifle Shot" and as "The Champion Shot of the World," and she could not let down either the assembled throng or Mr. Salsbury.

As Ringmaster Frank Richmond started to announce her act in his deep, melodic voice, Annie mounted her white horse. Bedecked in a cowboy hat, blouse with medals, and a short, pleated skirt specially designed so it would not become entangled in her legs, Annie hardly looked like an authentic Western character, but

Annie became one of the Wild West Show's main features, even though Annie had never lived in the West.

-31-

that was one of the features that attracted Buffalo Bill. He realized the audience contained a number of females, and he hoped that Annie's gentler appearance would make them feel more comfortable. He also placed Annie's act first. That way, if the women attendees saw that a tiny girl like Annie could easily handle a weapon, they would not be as frightened later when the bigger, louder guns rocked the arena.

"Ladies and Gentlemen!" boomed Richmond, "The Honorable William F. Cody and Nathan Salsbury present the feature attraction, unique and unparalleled, the foremost woman marksman in the world, in the exhibition of skill with the rifle, shotgun, and pistol—the little girl of the Western plains—Annie Oakley!"

Annie rode out to mild applause. A mounted cowboy joined her and, while galloping about the arena, tossed targets into the air. One by one Annie shattered the objects, drawing scattered applause each time. She then dismounted, aimed at a playing card thirty yards away with only the edge facing her, hit the card with one shot, then peppered it with holes as the card spun madly about the air. That feat drew louder applause.

Frank walked into the arena and placed a lighted cigarette in his mouth. From thirty yards, Annie knocked the ash off Frank's cigarette. More applause. Her next trick astounded the audience. As Frank twirled a small glass ball attached to a string around himself, Annie turned her back and looked carefully into a mirror. People gasped as they realized that she planned to shoot over her shoulder at her husband, relying only on the mirror as a guide!

A sudden stillness captured the stunned crowd as Annie peered into the mirror, steadied the rifle on her shoulder, then smashed the ball on her first attempt. Deafening cheers quickly drowned the noise of the gunshot as a grateful audience erupted in praise for this new talent. The next day, a newspaper stated that, "The largest share of applause was bestowed on Annie Oakley, a young girl whose proficiency with shotgun and rifle seems almost miraculous."

Strangely, since she came from a farming community, Annie felt at home with the Wild West Show, which turned into one of the world's most spectacular exhibitions. A splendid array of Western animals, such as buffalos, elk, bears, and bucking broncos, were joined by pony express riders, fierce-looking Indians wearing colorful warbonnets, robbers who held up a stagecoach in each performance, Mexican vaqueros, and unique characters like Con Groder, "Sheriff of the Platte," Buck Taylor, "King of the Cowboys," and Captain David C. Payne, "The Oklahoma Raider."

So much equipment and scenery, like the amazing canvas backdrop of the Rocky Mountains, accompanied the huge cast that Salsbury had to lease a special 26-car train to transport everything from show to show. The nation had seen little to compare with Buffalo Bill's Wild West Show, and fans flocked to take in its wondrous sights. Its stars became famous, including the little country girl from Ohio.

She loved working and traveling with the Show. Rougher characters, like authentic cowboys, took her under their wings and treated her like a daughter. When not performing, Annie loved to be around children of the other performers and make them laugh with one of her shooting tricks. She constantly practiced to add

Annie accumulated a trunkful of medals for her shooting exhibitions. Here she is pictured wearing some of them.

Besides her husband, Frank, possibly the one man Annie Oakley respected above all others was the famed Indian leader, Sitting Bull. The two struck up a close friendship during their time with Buffalo Bill's Wild West Show.

new twists to her routine and to make sure that her act did not grow stale. In that way, audiences would never know what to expect from Annie. They might see her shoot the flames off of a revolving wheel of candles, shoot at targets while lying on the back of a galloping horse, hit a dime in midair from thirty yards, or shatter a succession of glass balls that Frank tossed into the air. No matter what she did, thrilled audiences walked away talking about "Little Sure Shot, Wonder of the Age."

One man who never tired of watching Annie work her magic also grew quite fond of her. A featured attraction himself, he knew weapons and fighting like few people did, and thus appreciated what the girl could do with guns. Each time Annie took center stage that first year, he stopped what he was doing so he could take in the show. Sitting Bull, the Indian chief who had helped defeat General George Custer at the Little Bighorn and whose name once instilled terror in frontier communities, became Annie's biggest fan.

She returned the adoration, and soon a special relationship developed between the aging warrior and the young girl. Treating her as one of his own daughters, Sitting Bull spoke to her of things he never mentioned to others, such as his concern for the throngs of poor or abandoned children he noticed in many large cities.

One day he was speaking to Annie when a group of street children came by. "Look, Annie. The white man knows how to make everything, but he does not know how to distribute it. Why is it that in a land of so much wealth, so many children can go without?" As was his custom, Sitting Bull walked over to the children and handed them whatever change he had in his pockets.

"Sitting Bull was an open-handed uncle to every poor boy and girl he saw," mentioned Annie. "The contents of his pockets were often emptied into the hands of ragged little boys, nor could he understand how so much wealth could go brushing by, unmindful of the poor." Sitting Bull's compassion toward the less fortunate appealed to Annie, who had felt the bitter sting of mistreatment earlier in her life. A few years later, after U. S. cavalrymen had gunned down Sitting Bull out West, Annie received some of his most cherished possessions, such as his peace pipe, headdress, and a pair of moccasins he had worn at the Little Bighorn.

Moved by Sitting Bull's example, from then on Annie went out of her way to help needy children, whether by teaching sons and daughters of performers how to handle a weapon or by offering financial aid to an orphanage. One Sunday afternoon in New York, Annie and Frank went for a carriage ride through the city. As they turned one corner, Annie spotted a large group of children behind an iron fence.

"Stop the carriage, Frank. I want to get out."

Frank smiled lovingly at his wife, then reined in the horses. Annie scribbled a message on a piece of paper and walked over to the fence.

"Who's in charge here?" she asked one of the children. When an adult superviser responded, Annie handed him the note inviting every boy and girl in the orphanage to the next day's show. For a few hours at least, compliments of Annie's charitable heart, a group of young people laughed and yelled in glee rather than thought of where they lived. For the rest of her life, Annie tried to help orphans whenever she could.

With few exceptions, those first two years with Buffalo Bill passed happily. In 1886 she became seriously ill in New York when a severe case of blood poisoning infected one of her ears. After a specialist lanced the ear, a dangerously high fever set in. Annie tossed and turned for three days before the fever broke. In a seventeen-year career covering 170,000 miles of travel and thousands of shows, the only four she missed occurred during this crisis.

The appearance in New York in the summer of 1886 drew such large crowds and made so much money that Cody and his partners rented Madison Square Garden for a winter run. An enormous backdrop of the Rockies was added, complete with green forests and towering mountains, as was a powerful wind machine strong enough to blow a stagecoach across the arena. The most anticipated addition, however, was the stunning re-creation of "Custer's Last Fight, the Battle of the Little Bighorn," which captivated audiences at each performance. Many famous people attended among the one million who paid to see the show, such as Civil War General William T. Sherman, circus showman P. T. Barnum, and Custer's widow.

One spectator was so excited by what he saw that he wrote a fan letter to Cody suggesting he take the Show overseas. Mark Twain, author of such famous novels as *Tom Sawyer* and *Huckleberry Finn*, urged, "It is often said that none of the exhibitions we send to England are purely and distinctly American. If you will take the Wild West Show over there you can remove that criticism."

Thus, based on the Show's astounding suc-

cess and the advice of a novelist, Annie Oakley was about to cross the ocean and tour Europe. The little girl was heading worlds away from her simple beginnings in Ohio.

Perhaps because she had such a tumultuous childhood, Annie frequently paid for children to attend the Wild West Show and would often stop at orphanages to offer help.

TRIUMPH IN ENGLAND

The hustle and bustle along the wharves of New York Harbor on March 31, 1887, surprised even veteran dock workers. They had seen hundreds of ships loaded with all sorts of cargo, but they had never watched such a wide variety of supplies and people stream onto a ship as the conglomerationthat poured onto the steamship, *State of Nebraska.* Cowboys stepped aboard with Indians, buffalos followed closely on the heels of horses, and trunk after trunk of equipment filled the ship's hold.

The Wild West Show was heading across the Atlantic Ocean to England to join in the festivities being held to honor Queen Victoria's Golden Jubilee—her 50th year as Queen of the country. Since all of Europe's rulers and important people planned to travel to the London area

Annie, here wearing Scottish clothing, was as big a hit in Europe as she was back home.

As always throughout her career, Annie practiced hard to keep her skills at top level. Here she shoots targets as some Native American members of the Show look on.

sometime during the spring or summer of 1887, as did practically every English citizen, Cody had a ready market for his show.

Annie could barely contain her excitement over the ocean voyage. Other than a few quick crossings of rivers and small lakes, the twenty-six-year-old Annie had spent her entire life on land, and now here she was about to head out onto the immense Atlantic!

As the steamship departed from New York, Annie watched in fascination from the main deck. Other performers preferred staying in their cabins below decks, but not Annie. Like a child staring at a shiny new toy, Annie took in everything she could, not just that first day, but each day in the voyage.

Before the ship had been on the ocean three days, almost everybody in the show was moaning in the cabins with seasickness, including Buffalo Bill. Despite the weather, though, Annie remained on deck, unaffected by the rolling of the steamship and huge waves that sometimes crashed over the deck. One time the ship's skipper, Captain Braes, muttered to Annie, "I thought the whole Wild West was battened down. But you look pleased, Miss Oakley."

"It's my first time out of sight of land!" she exclaimed in excitement.

On the seventh day, a particularly heavy sea so captivated Annie that she later wrote to a friend, "I learned the power of the mighty waves. It was a glorious sight, our boat being dashed from side to side; I felt that one foot farther and we would be turned bottom-side up." Yet she remained on the main deck while nature howled about her. Alone of all the Wild West cast members, Annie spotted the coast of Europe on the twelfth day with bittersweet feelings.

Annie and the rest of the cast received an indication from one of their first shows that their stay in England would be a major success. Queen Victoria, who had rarely been seen in public since her husband's death twenty-five years earlier, requested a command performance on May 11. She intended to remain for only one hour, but the Queen so enjoyed the spectacle that she watched the entire presentation. Afterward she asked to meet the cast, and when Annie approached her, the Queen mentioned that she was "a very clever little girl." Before leaving, Queen Victoria asked that a second command performance be scheduled so that she could invite all of the foreign dignitaries who were in London, such as the Kings of Denmark, Greece, and Sweden, and the King and Queen of Belgium.

The Wild West Show drew capacity crowds and became the talk of England. Of all the stars, none stood out as much as Annie, who dazzled England with her shooting exhibitions and her good manners. She received numerous party invitations, and the London Gun Club, a male-dominated organization, presented her with a stunning rifle bearing a tiny gold figure of herself set into the stock. A constant stream of flowers and letters of admiration deluged her tent, which was normally besieged by visitors. Annie cheerfully greeted each person and made everyone feel at home in her spacious accommodations.

"After the exciting performance," wrote one London newspaper reporter, "we sought the peaceful seclusion of Miss Annie Oakley's tent, where she charmingly served us various American juices of choice and agreeable flavor."

She so bewitched the English that four men, unaware that Annie already had a husband, asked to marry her. One suitor included his picture with the proposal, which Frank pinned to a wall. Annie smiled, picked up her rifle, and punctured the man's head with a series of well-placed shots. The two then mailed back the picture.

Of all the notes, letters, and invitations, Annie only kept one. George Widows, 21, attended each show specifically to watch Annie's act. He wanted to meet her, but the shy young man could not summom the courage to approach her tent. Instead, he fell in love from a distance.

The news that Annie already was married crushed Widows, who became so distressed that he arranged to leave England. Before he departed, Widows mailed a lengthy letter to Annie in which he finally poured out his feelings.

He described how Annie had touched his heart with "your grace, your gentle bearing, and your sweet face with your expressive eyes that look out from under that broad-brimmed hat so becomingly worn." He touched Annie by relating that "I lost my father when I was a very small boy and my mother, who is of gentle birth, brought me up very close to her. So you see my worldly experiences have been limited." He closed by telling Annie that he could not bear being near London and was leaving for Africa that very day.

This moving letter so affected Annie that she kept it the rest of her life. Twenty-five years later, in 1912, Widows visited Annie and Frank at their Chesapeake Bay home and reminisced about the incident.

Not each note contained a marriage proposal. One even caused stress between Annie and Cody. The Prince of Wales wrote Annie a letter asking if she would meet the Grand Duke Michael of Russia in a shooting contest. The grand duke was in London to celebrate the

Annie received numerous medals and awards for her exhibitions in Europe.

Jubilee and to seek the hand of Queen Victoria's daughter in marriage. As he fancied himself an expert marksman, he also eagerly sought a challenge with Annie.

The Prince of Wales was delighted to arrange the match, since he felt certain Annie would defeat the grand duke. Few people in England, including the prince, liked the Russian and prayed that nothing would come of his efforts to marry their princess. Maybe if he lost a shooting match with a woman, reasoned the Prince of Wales, he would leave.

Though Grand Duke Michael could shoot well, he was no equal to Annie, who easily defeated him. A dejected Michael quickly returned to Russia. The English press jubilantly stated in banner headlines that Annie had decided two matches—the shooting contest and the marriage question. "It was the most amazing and unexpected publicity I ever experienced," wrote Annie, who became an even bigger hero in England.

The incident caused problems with Buffalo Bill, though, who felt that his star marksman had publicly humiliated the grand duke. Cody had already voiced his displeasure that Annie had earlier shaken hands with the Princess Alexandra rather than bowing and kissing the back of her hand, as called for by proper etiquette, and he had become more enraged—and jealous—over Annie's soaring popularity in England. It was his show, and Cody was bothered that one of his workers was stealing most of the publicity.

Thus when the London show closed after a successful run—two and a half million people attended—and Cody rented an indoor arena near Manchester for the winter, Annie and Frank left the Wild West Show to go off on their own. They hated to leave what had been such a happy world, but Cody's bitterness made it too hard to remain.

For a few months the two hunted at a friend's estate near London, then traveled to Germany at the invitation of Crown Prince Wilhelm, who asked Annie to stage a shooting exhibition for him. The exhibition proceeded smoothly until the portion where Annie planned to shoot the ashes off a cigarette placed in Frank's mouth. As she prepared for the event, Crown Prince Wilhelm leapt to the front and asked to take Frank's place.

"I did not want to use him as a target, for what if I missed?" wondered Annie. Wilhelm was in line to be Germany's next ruler, and she could imagine what the reaction would be if she hurt, or worse—killed—Wilhelm.

When a prince invites you to his country, then asks a favor, you do it. Annie aimed, muttered a quick prayer, and fired. Wilhelm stepped back with a shattered cigarette, a smile, and no injury.

Following this exhibition, Annie and Frank headed for home. They were tired, probably a little homesick, and disheartened over the rift with Cody.

They arrived in the United States shortly before Christmas 1887, and after a brief vacation they toured the country, completing a string of exhibitions for shooting clubs or large theaters. For a short time they even joined a competing show called Pawnee Bill's Frontier Exhibition, but they missed the large crowds and applause generated by Buffalo Bill's Wild West

Show. It had become home to them; the workers had become family. Annie and Frank longed
to return.

BACK TO THE WILD WEST

In the spring of 1889 a surprise visitor called on Annie and Frank. Nate Salsbury hoped to persuade Annie to rejoin the Wild West Show for its upcoming three-year tour of Europe.

"We miss you, Missie," he began. "The Colonel and I want you back. The show is going to Paris for the Exposition celebrating the one hundreth anniversary of the French Revolution. It won't be the same without you."

The words seemed like music to Annie's ears. Apparently Buffalo Bill had forgotten the previous year's incidents and hated to go back to Europe without one of his most popular acts, so Salsbury had arrived to smooth things over. A delighted Annie immediately accepted.

The tour opened in Paris in May 1889 and quickly captured the hearts of Parisians. Though enthralled by the strange conglomera-

Annie decorated her tent with many luxuries and reminders of home. For years, tents and hotel rooms were the only homes the couple enjoyed.

tion of animals, outlaws, and cavalrymen that were uniquely American, Parisians warmed to Annie like no other member. Jubilantly shouting, "Long live Annie Oakley! Long live Annie Oakley!" the French population resounded in cheers with each display of marksmanship. They roared when Annie jumped onto her white horse, snared a pistol from the ground while riding by, then demolished six targets tossed in the air before they hit the dirt. They applauded when her bullets snuffed out lighted candles without damaging the candle itself.

Some spectators doubted what they saw. At one Paris show, a man from the audience yelled to Annie to prove she was actually hitting the targets with her bullets. Some people had been duped by supposed marksmen in other touring shows who used blanks, while an assistant rang bells indicating hit after hit.

"Do you have a pocket watch, sir?" inquired Annie. When he replied that he did, she added, "If you are not sure that I am using real bullets, let me use it for a target."

The Frenchman paused, then handed his possession forward. Frank took the watch, which was attached to a chain, twirled the piece over his head, and waited. Before he had spun the timepiece five times, it burst into pieces. The humbled Frenchman offered his apology to Annie, who graciously agreed to replace the destroyed watch.

As in England, Annie's tent hosted a steady stream of visitors. Though she received no further marriage proposals, well-wishers came by to greet her and fans poured in to chat with her. They found as many of the comforts of home as Annie could possibly fit into the tent, including a beautiful rocking chair, colorful carpeting covering the dreary floorboard, cushions placed atop trunks, and bright flowers. Frank's travel desk and a folded canvas bathtub stood off to the side, while warbonnets, medals, rifles, and photographs covered each wall.

One visitor made one of the most peculiar requests Annie ever received. The King of Senegal was so impressed after watching Annie's performance that he approached Annie after the show. "I wish to buy Mademoiselle Oakley," he said in a serious tone as he mentioned an amount. Cody, who stood next to his shooting star, stifled an urge to smile and politely replied that he could not accept. Frank did not know whether to laugh at this apparent attempt to steal his wife away or to challenge the man.

"I will increase my offer," the king countered. When Cody still declined, the ruler explained why he wanted Annie. "There are wild animals threatening my villages. They are killing people. I need you and wish to buy you."

A relieved Cody, with Frank and Annie now grinning at his side, told the king that Annie's time was already so filled that she could not possibly take a leave and travel to his country. What at first looked like an embarrassing situation turned into a rather humorous event.

Other parts of the tour did not bring a smile to Annie's face. In Barcelona, Spain, her heart went out to poor, starving Spaniards who scavenged the Show's garbage for bits of food. However, in doing so, the hungry people exposed Cody's entire group to deadly influenza and smallpox, which forced the Spanish government to place the performers in quarantine—they could not leave their living areas nor could any show be scheduled. Ringmaster Frank Richmond and thirteen other workers died before Cody con-

Well-wishers and fans frequently stopped by Annie's tent in hopes in seeing the famous entertainer.

tracted a steamer to take them away from Spain.

The Show moved on to Austria, where Annie met the nation's emperor in 1890. Always sensitive to others as a result of her own harsh childhood, Annie instantly detected a sadness in the monarch. "I really felt sorry when I looked into the face of the Emperor of Austria. His face looked both tired and troubled. I then and there decided that being just plain little Annie Oakley, with ten minutes work once or twice a day, was good enough for me, for I had, or at least I thought I had, my freedom."

When a wealthy woman in Vienna, Austria asked Annie to arrange a show for orphans, Annie readily agreed. The successful performance not only entertained many children, which warmed Annie, but raised a large amount of money for the orphanage. To show her appreciation, the wealthy woman sent Annie a bag filled with gold coins. Without a thought, Annie handed the money to the orphanage, a gesture that so touched the Austrian woman that she had a special diamond pin handcrafted for Annie.

When the lengthy tour ended in 1892, a weary Annie and Frank returned to the United States. After eight years on the road with Buffalo Bill, the couple believed they were ready to finally purchase something they could call home, so they acquired a comfortable house in Nutley, New Jersey. However, since their work took them on the road for at least seven months each year, they eventually sold the home.

Annie and Frank continued to enjoy their work with Buffalo Bill, even though the constant travel wore them down. A successful 1893 run in Chicago, Illinois kept the Show in heavy demand for most of the next decade, and as always Annie received as much joy entertaining or helping children as she did amazing the capacity crowds.

One newcomer to the Show, marksman Johnny Baker, was Cody's foster son. Annie spent hours coaching him in the fine points of shooting. Her words, repeated numerous times, made an impression on the eager youth. "Practice, practice, practice, and always believe in yourself," Annie told Baker. "Don't try too hard, though, or you'll get too tense. Coordination is the important thing."

As Baker improved, he loved challenging his instructor to a shooting match, but he never could defeat Annie. Some newspaper reporters thought Baker was purposely losing all the time just to make Annie look good, but he denied it. "There never was a day when I didn't try to beat her, but it just couldn't be done."

It appeared nothing could slow down the amazing Annie. In 1901, however, her long string of good fortune came to a sudden end.

"NEVER A MORE LOVEABLE WOMAN"

October 28, 1901, lifted everyone's spirits in the Wild West Show. Not only had the Charlotte, North Carolina performance been a rousing success—12,000 people attended—but only one more stop remained before they could all go home for a much-needed winter rest. The cast, including Annie and Frank, piled onto the train bound for Danville, Virginia, in a lighthearted mood.

As the train neared Lexington, Virginia later that night, the startled engineer blinked down the tracks in disbelief. Charging straight at them from the opposite direction was a second train. A loud screech split the nighttime silence and woke sleeping passengers as both engineers futilely tried to stop tons of speeding metal in a short distance. Annie started out of her bed, but a sudden jolt tumbled her backwards. A

The wear and tear of constant life on the road failed to show in Annie's face, which remained vibrant and alive.

frightful grinding noise drowned out other sounds as the trains crashed head on into each other.

"Are you all right!" yelled Frank into the darkness of their cabin. "Annie, where are you?"

"I'm all right, Frank. I'm over here," responded Annie with a weakened voice. Her husband scrambled in the darkness until he located her, then tenderly carried her out of the train and placed her on the ground.

They could hardly believe what they saw. Miraculously, no one was killed, but injured workers and numerous dead or dying show animals dotted the landscape. Some members of the crew were already walking about the tracks with rifles, putting the injured animals out of their misery. Cody, looking pale and weak, stumbled around in a daze.

The conductor of freight train Number 75, heading south, had missed a signal informing him about Cody's train. Instead of moving to a side track, the conductor continued on the main rail, unaware that he was speeding straight toward disaster. Cody lost almost one hundred horses in the accident.

Annie needed immediate medical attention, for the wreck had caused internal injuries, paralyzed her left side, and badly cut her right leg. She required months of rehabilitation in St. Michael's Hospital in Newark, New Jersey, including many operations, before doctors released her. Wearing a brace on her leg and hobbling with the aid of a cane, Annie finally left to recuperate in a New Jersey home that Frank had purchased for her comfort.

The Show continued in the spring, but Annie was unable to accompany it because of her injuries. Over the next ten years she made

few public appearances. In 1902 she took the role of Nance Berry, the leading character in a drama called *The Western Girl*. In the play Annie, as Berry, deftly used a rifle, pistol, and rope to foil a notorious group of outlaws called the Silver Creek bandits. With Annie as its featured attraction, the drama successfully toured the East.

Mainly, though, she and Frank were more content to enjoy their home and let Annie fully recover from her injuries. Her fans felt otherwise. One reporter asked in his newspaper column, "Where, oh, where is Annie Oakley? It does not seem quite the same old shooting match without Miss Oakley potting pigeons in

Though the accident slowed Annie down, she still hunted on occasion.

When her close friend Buffalo Bill asked Annie to rejoin the Show for one final tour in 1912, Annie agreed without hesitation.

the ring."

In 1912, when Cody announced that year's version would be his final tour, Annie rejoined in honor of her friend. Though she could not move as easily as before the accident, she was still superb at shooting, and her compassion touched others as deeply as always.

"There was never a sweeter, gentler, more lovable woman than Annie Oakley," declared one man who worked with Annie during this time.

Following that tour, Annie led a fairly quiet existence. The Carolina Hotel, an elegant resort for wealthy people in Pinehurst, North Carolina, hired her to give lessons to its customers. While Frank managed the skeet range, Annie taught numerous hotel guests how to shoot, including such famous Americans as oil producer John D. Rockefeller, popularizer of musical marches John Philip Sousa, and novelist Booth Tarkington. When World War I erupted in 1917, she traveled to Army training centers, where she put on exhibitions for the troops and joked that she had shot the wrong end off the cigarette of Crown Prince Wilhelm back in 1887—the same Wilhelm who was now leader of the German enemy.

The years were winding down for Annie, though. Friends from her past had died, disappeared, or drifted to other locations. Memories occupied more of her time, which saddened the normally smiling entertainer. She received a jolt in 1917 when news of Buffalo Bill's death reached her. "Goodbye, old friend," she wrote in a telegraph message. "The setting sun beyond the western hills will pay daily tribute to the last great pioneer of the West."

At her doctor's request, the 62-year-old

Annie and her husband moved to Florida in 1922 to take advantage of the warmer climate. Driving to their home in Leesburg, Florida, however, Annie sustained further injuries when the car hit a soft stretch in the road and toppled over. A fractured hip and broken ankle slowed an already-weakened woman.

Four years later, desiring to spend her final days in familiar surroundings, Annie moved home to Ohio and her beloved fields and family. Newer forms of entertainment and younger stars that burst forth in an era called "The Roaring Twenties" overshadowed Annie and other performers of the Wild West Show, so she lived quietly, content to pass time with Frank and other family.

One day famed comedian Will Rogers visited Annie in Dayton. Afterward, unsettled by Annie's frail health and downcast spirit, he wrote a stirring article in his national newspaper column about the former star.

"This is a good story about a little woman that all the older generation will remember. She was the reigning sensation of America and Europe during the heyday of Buffalo Bill's Wild West Show. She was their star. I had heard cowboys who had traveled with the Bill Show speak of her almost in reverence. They loved her."

He explained that her picture had looked down from more billboards than current Hollywood actresses and that she was "the greatest woman rifle shot the world has ever produced. Nobody took her place. There is only one."

He then got to his point. "She is bedridden from an automobile accident a few years ago. I want you to write her, all you who remember her, and those that can, go and see her." His

In her final years, Annie could rarely enjoy the hobbies that had once been such a large part of her life.

Frank Butler, left, followed his beloved wife in death by only twenty days.

readers responded with an affection that touched both Annie and Frank, who happily read the hundreds of telegrams and letters that poured into their home.

Later that year, on November 3, 1926, Annie Oakley died in her sleep in Dayton, Ohio. Almost as if he were only waiting for Annie to give the cue, Frank passed away twenty days later.

Annie Oakley reigned as one of the nation's top entertainers for more than twenty years. More than that, though, her compassionate attitude toward the less fortunate, especially children, left a legacy for all.

Will Rogers said it best. "She was a marvelous woman, kindest hearted, most thoughtful, a wonderful Christian woman. I doubt if her character could be matched anywhere outside of a saint. Annie Oakley's name, her lovable traits, her thoughtful consideration of others, will live as a mark for any woman to shoot at."

CHRONOLOGY

August 13, 1860	Annie Moses (Oakley) is born in Darke County, Ohio.
1866	Annie's father, Jacob Moses, dies.
1867	Annie's sister, Mary Jane, dies.
1869	Annie is sent to the Darke County Infirmary.
1870-1872	Annie spends two miserable years with Mr. and Mrs. "wolf".
1872	Annie returns to her mother.
1873-1876	Annie's hunting makes money for the family.
1876	Annie moves to Cincinnati.
1879	Annie defeats Frank Butler in a shooting match.
1880	Annie marries Frank Butler.
1880-1885	Annie and Frank tour the Midwest.
1884	Annie and Frank sign with the Sells Brothers Circus.
1885	Annie signs with Buffalo Bill's Wild West Show.
1886	Annie is seriously ill with food poisoning.
March 31, 1887	Annie heads to Europe with the Wild West Show.
May 11, 1887	Annie meets Queen Victoria after a command performance.
December, 1887	Annie and Frank return to the United States.
Spring, 1889	Annie rejoins the Wild West Show.
May, 1889	Second European tour opens in Paris.
1892	Annie and Frank return to the United States.
October 29, 1901	Annie is seriously injured in a train wreck.
1912	Annie rejoins Buffalo Bill for his final Wild West tour.
1917	Buffalo Bill dies.
1917-1918	Annie puts on shooting exhibitions for troops during World War I.
1922	Annie and Frank move to Florida.
1922	Annie is injured in an automobile accident.
November 3, 1926	Annie Oakley dies at age 66.
November 23, 1926	Frank Butler dies.

Havighurst, Walter. *Annie Oakley of the Wild West.* Lincoln: University of Nebraska Press, 1992.

————. *Buffalo Bill's Great Wild West Show.* New York: Random House, 1957.

Kirk, Rhina. *Circus Heroes and Heroines.* New York: Hammond Inc.,1972.

Levine, Ellen. *Ready, Aim, Fire!: The Real Adventures of Annie Oakley.* New York: Scholastic, Inc., 1989.

McLoughlin, Denis. *Wild & Wooly: An Encyclopedia of the Old West.* Garden City, New York: Doubleday & Company, Inc., 1975.

O'Neil, Paul. *The Old West: The End and the Myth.* Alexandria, Virginia: Time-Life Books, 1979.

Raven, Susan, and Alison Weir. *Women of Achievement.* New York: Harmony Books, 1981.

Wayne, Bennett, Editor. *Women Who Dared to Be Different.* Champaign, Illinois: Garrard Publishing Company, 1973.

INDEX

ABOUT THE AUTHOR

John F. Wukovits is a teacher and writer from Trenton, Michigan, who specializes in history and sports. His work has appeared in more than 25 national publications, including *Wild West* and *America's Civil War*. His books include a biography of the World War II commander Admiral Clifton Sprague, and he has written biographies of Barry Sanders, Jesse James, and Wyatt Earp for Chelsea House. A graduate of the University of Notre Dame, Wukovits is the father of three daughters—Amy, Julie, and Karen.